Windows Facing East

Windows Facing East

Caroline Finkelstein

DRAGON GATE, INC.
PORT TOWNSEND, WASHINGTON

Grateful acknowledgment is made to the following publications in which some of these poems first appeared: *Ironwood Press, Green House, The Antioch Review, The Yale Literary Magazine, Intro 10, The Bennington Review, Harvard Magazine, The Little Magazine, Fire House, Poetry, Tendril,* and *Ploughshares.*

Grateful acknowledgment is made to the National Endowment for the Arts and the Vermont Council on the Arts. The author and the publisher wish to express their gratitude to the Literature Program of the National Endowment for the Arts for additional grant support, which greatly assisted the publication of this book.

Fierce gratitude to my teachers, my children, and to Robert Clinton.

Designed by Tree Swenson.
The type, Electra, was designed by W. A. Dwiggins.

Library of Congress Cataloging-in-Publication Data

Finkelstein, Caroline.
Windows facing east.

Poems.
I. Title.
PS3556.I4827W5 1986 811'.54 85-27580
ISBN 0-937872-30-X
ISBN 0-937872-31-8 (pbk.)

Dragon Gate, Inc.
508 Lincoln Street
Port Townsend
Washington 98368

To my mother

Contents

I

II

I

For the old, the wasted bodies
with their memories of succulence,
for those who play the radio, the luckless
and the lucky prospector, the lovers
entirely original in nakedness,
for the culpable, including children
and the horse who stands for breeding,
for oceanographers and whales and whelks
netted by mistake and pulled to sassy decks
that yaw, flirting with the weather,
then scare and right themselves –

for the brambles' viciousness and fruit
that urges on the hungry birds a diligence
so admirable, for fierce conquistadors
of undiscovered stars –
comes death, a stranger grave and fallen
to this endless task, whispering, as orphans do,
of a homeland beautifully imagined and of father.

Of the eyes, the feathering brows,
he writes most.
The body, fully broken, is bleeding,
laid out on the stationmaster's table,
while the eyes remain the same beautiful
and unseeing black,
as if to drive home the blindness in desire.
                                        You wonder what he feels
as from his study window he watches her
approaching up the lane of poplars
in her little boots, the ripening beneath
her coat of fur and wool,
and why he turns back, raging, to the page:
arranging the soot in all of Russia
to fall on that flesh the train crushes
and spoils.

Grandfather had died;
after the season I was sent to Auntie.
Margaret was there. I felt rather proud
of mourning but forgot my sorrow;
they filled my room with roses.
For evening they carved the swans
in ice and composed the fruit; the sky,
as we went in to dinner, borrowed the color
of my watered silk cloak.
I smiled most at Edward.
In bed, so late, I heard owls hooting
near my window as Margaret came, quietly,
down the stone hall. No one could have heard –
I think I shall never hear those birds again
without thinking of the flax along her skin –
I am sure to marry Edward.
The neighborhood is hot and full of bees.
Afternoons it cools; I love the way
the thunder comes.

She dreams he beats her.
Her flesh sags on her face
where he put his fists
yet she seems oddly pretty
as if bruise were ornament: those yellows
and those blues.
But the real cause is damage in the bone,
a past: never any meat but always
the overloaded glass, lukewarm rivulets
of cream clotting in her throat.
She dreams her own refusal –
now her mother's cool reflection
on the rim.

Running my fingers up
the green shoots, feeling for the bud,
knowing the right light and water
will empower the stalks to bloom
starry-white, fragrant,

I prepare the beds, Canton bowls
filled with rough gravel
of no distinctive color, and watch
by a winter window,
cleaning the tip of green,
an issue of the heart come through the stalk.

There is nothing
written on the package of bulbs
to indicate their politics.
They want nothing
but water and the cold north light
to push upward.
They are nothing
but promises of wild scented arrangements

and I force them.

No longer need man envy the birds,
says a child's book on flight,
... *we venture into space in foil suits.*
When the cancer peaked,
they dressed him in clothes
designed for the moon.

Your chickadee,
who loved the yew's bright beads,
lit on the brick walk
repeating his name –
dee, dee, dee,
and the sun polishing his cap.

His bones have hollowed out
but he resists, you hear
breaking when he calls, you damn
your ears. Worse. Worse
than anything,
you take the feeder down.

There is reason for this control.
The neighbor blamed the air
for what happened to her child,
her lack of vigilance. I hear
she does not sleep.
We shall have order in this house:
we will watch the birds
and not bicker in the yard.
                    At night, after you've done your teeth,
climb, clean, into my lap
where I shall count your bones,
each fringing lash.
When I cut you with my tongue,
I am checking on your blood.
I will not have it going white.

Was it fear of his disciplined body
or the light, unreadable look in his eyes
that finally exhausted her?
I barely see the Belgian lace she wore
as she lingered
delicate on his arm,
a plume in a Junker's helmet

while Grandpa, bankrupt in America,
waited her arrival.
Those springlike nights:
as the train whistle mixes with locusts,
does she feel the breath of the dogs
guarding the boxcars;
does she see that terrible cargo –
to leave Berlin, carrying grief like a figurine?

Pulls her obi tight,
tonight she'll use the lute –
displays her wrists, the little feet
marking time and the lacquered hair
above the nape.
How long it's gone this way,
filling up the tubs, the multiple
cups of wine –
when free she works her countryside
in silk: stitches a hill
where women bundle firewood.
Gentlemen, do you wish to see the lotus
so entwined? My brother seeks a doctor
for his coughing. They say, in the mountains,
cedars weep as prettily as maids.

The generale walks among us,
he who could ride in his open car
anywhere unhindered,
he who could command one thousand horsemen
to dismount and scour the sea
or any woman to scream for his salt
or decree that every third child
blind a donkey for his character;
he is powerful is he not,
and yet he walks among us

and the parrots burden the air,
here the coqs rip at their cages
while the sun beats up the dust on the fronds
that overhang the avenues, the wide streets
where we are walking maybe dreaming together
of his immaculate head stamped on our coins
and how magnificent our bodies would be
covered in gilt and undulant braid,
how splendid we would seem to the crowds,
would we not,
and to that man looking hard at us,
as if to remember in what village we had met,
in what courtyard we had lingered
those hot afternoons
handing round the fruit.

I have spent my whole life lying down,
she wrote.
In her room: the thin hum of wire
in the hours before they came
and outside a whole people,
still, on provided benches.
He took her in a birch grove,
blood printed in snow;
then the last birch was seen
from a window of the northern train.
There were beds but nobody slept
as she remembers their question:
Is this your child?
and when they didn't ask it anymore.

Imagine this life

how she brews tea in her flat,
how from time to time she's sent a little sugar.

TODAY IS THE ANNIVERSARY OF THE INVENTION OF BARBED WIRE

And I plan to return to the desert.
So much arid heat but so little commotion,
not one volume of Voltaire,
no need to learn compassion for city planners,
no tumultuous markets set up in front of churches,
no high church, nothing Byzantine, nothing
Florentine, nothing tooled in leather,
no wallets, no cases for a watch
straight out of Berne, no trolley, no Einstein
on his way to work so bored he changes time,

no special breeds of horses posted
outside special places, no conceptions, recipes, awesome
predilections requiring things that hurt,
no history of letters and before that
the need to make crusades, no grooms
drunk on mead and stumbling over homicides
throughout the forest, no forest, ash
and maple falling silent into loam –

and I plan to make it perfect.
Me, at ease without motors and fables,
me, content with a plain cup
there on the flat horizon, believing
there is no circle
and not ringing my well with barbed wire
against animals or the inevitable stranger
cunning always and thirsty.

My father is dead,
my mother is watching the clock
as I come into the room
too late to see her bending across his chest.
I have the feeling that this has happened before.
Her only daughter,
I haven't the heart to soothe
having broken down earlier.
She is watching the clock,
underwater she is watching the growth
of her hair on forming fish and screaming
It is no dream
and I don't have it in me to blame
when they enter with needles
to which she gives
the whole of her desperate body.

She has quit the little garden
and a rose from her bodice
falls to the muddy drive.

Waiting out the rain,
two peasants talk about the rebel
to be hanged at noon.
It is luck, they say,
to have rope cut from the noose,
to have it in the house.

When she finds the rose
returned to the table,
she casts it in the hearth.
I understand that she is also burned

as I understand she never knew the man
and planned a trip to Paris in the month,
taking with her the maid who is a cousin
to the fellow hungry for the rope.

In Paris, Turgenev, dying
lonely as a finger, and cold,
scribbles by the fire, sometimes heavy lines,
sometimes drawing garlands on the border.

The elements conspire:
who can tell what century it is
in snow before the plow
or in the later months
when the garden, rife with scent,
phlox and heliotrope, is an exile's garden?

Her legacies conspire:
she has inherited a Russian olive tree.
She often sits beneath its limbs
humming to herself, in sadness
imagines things different:
the house replaced
with what she cannot arrange
or how she would slacken her carriage
to lean into him and the roses
crushing beneath them.

She has lately been to the bank.
There was Pushkin sweating, no,
it was the cavalry officer, no,
it was just the doctor, someone
very tired.

You play with her sash,
she calls her dog Duchess, lets loose
her hair, and longs for you with her smile.
She has inherited her body.

The gypsies were dirty, right, Grandma,
and ate anything.
Nothing grows in your yard
although the man next door has grapes,
blue on the vine, and flowers.
I hear him singing
or is it the German officer
who so admires you that sings,
or nameless birds, or women
braiding bread: the hushed thud of that dough —
the neighbor offers zucchini you take to throw away.
There's more of the gypsies: at nighttime,
you tell what they did with their dogs.

In my Italian movie
the weeds of yarrow
are called Pearly Everlasting
& the light is pure Turner:
all soft rose off the Adriatic.
We sit on the piazza
drinking Campari & soda,
smoking a little
Turkish dope
& very gently
your supple leather
touches mine
the slow warm way
& the priest slyly pulls the bells.
So why do you jump up
like a desperado about to rob the stage?
Why do you tuck in your studded shirt,
buckle up your gun belt
& make one fast grab
for my dance-hall tits?
I said this was an *Italian* movie,
blue eyes.

Oh and a real love and also an umbrella,
green and white, big enough to sit under
with our drinks of gin and lime
and a perfect dramatic rendition
where all of the actors bring tears
yet you go away light-headed, better
for the pathos, the cherry orchard standing,
also the silks not fraying
and later him saying: *silk*,
he is touching the top of my leg,
he says *silk* and then he says *water*,
and the clams on the plate are cooling
and the fork beside the plate is absolutely clean
and pronged like a silver trident,
and if irony eats with us, Godmother,
we offer a glass of wine
before we pierce that gorgeous throat
and rip and skin and gnaw.

At the last I read you Chekhov
near the garden. It was so hot
the writing blurred, and the girl
sequestered by her sister wore a sash
the very blue of the chicory you tore.
The artist in the story bought ink
but never drew; it was summer in the book
but would be fall
by the time you staked the beans.

Bees were everywhere, anxious for the queen;
you flung the hoe –
and now the real pain begins,
for the artist leaves the girl
and takes the midnight train. Effects no rescue.
Will paint, in Moscow, rich girls for their fathers.

Bleeding on board the steamer,
Chekhov commits these endings,
coughs into his fine linen cloth.

The leaves are burning
and our voices are full of data.
Here are the apples
we gathered in the orchard,
and here the goblets copying,
in their clear swell, our faces.
We handle business at the table.
Afraid, we talk in code.

See how the candlesmoke replicates
the paintings of the caves:
the antelope's belly and plush,
the back's magical hollows
and the sacrifice.

for Nicholas

Burdock grows where plum and pear
once stood; burdock feeds the snails.
The snails, contented, say
the rain is made to fall
so the burdock leaves will grow
large as a lady's apron. They say
the same of sunlight.

The avenue of limes,
given up entirely to burdock,
is remembered by the snails
as where the manor lord would view
his peasants harvesting the wheat.
When it was very hot,
the girls sponged their brothers.

The garden wall is mostly broken stone.
Burdock flourishes nearby,
pushing through the fissures
in the mortar. The snails, contented,
tell stories to each other
in the dusk, stories of rich marriages
and feasts, those days when men shook the woods
for snails to cook till they grew black,
then laid on silver dishes.
They try to imagine the honor
of being placed on a silver dish.
For our sakes, they say, sun shines
on burdock leaves and we are happy
when it rains. Burdock covers over
all the garden.

Thank you for the roses.
I've put them in the special vase,
you know, the one with figures
done in white and blue:
stationed flying geese, so Japanese,
and just below the lip
a swelling curve I've filled with water.
I've put them in the coolest room
to keep them from blooming
straight off and dropping pollen
in which to trace the letters of my name.
Aren't you pleased
with this arrangement? Did you,
for instance, want it otherwise,
in full sun, say, opening like crazy...

Ah, Mama, we are in Russia.
The tremendous fall of snow curves
the already curving roof; out front
the bays are matched. They stamp in icy air.
Or it is warmer: summering in the country
we glow. And pale in the shade, like petals.

I am that child watching
you anticipate the night to come
at Madame B.'s, the programme there,
the menu specialty, and one
precise sensualist
so attached to mirrors and his title.

Lately come from the gypsies,
only laughter is in his eyes, one girl
was naked on a horse.
The birches bend like women.
He touches you just above the wrist
while violins, screened behind the fronds,
play on and on. Songs to break your heart.

II

She cannot say
this mess with the hens and ducks is life.
And there is nothing in her cup of coffee
that beats her dream of Paraguay: a girl
practicing sternness on her way to school.
In the empty kitchen, steam becomes fabulous
jacaranda. Her butter slicks the bellies
of the colonels' famous wives.

And to her the yard is Prague, the barn
a visa stamping *yes* on yesterday's ballroom.
Someone waltzes in the stalls. Under the posts
that become the lindens, linden flowers fall
as nuns would fall, conspicuous in silence.
She read novels as a child.

She feeds the birds. She cannot say
this is a sparrow only, this is a nest
made with creek mud and feathers slowly
with positive cheer. Alone and small
she called in the night *hello*.
Now a cedar is a castle. On or off the wall
a man is a valentine.
And in the fortress of excuse
geese fly into a sky of gray paper—
specks of nothing but rue.

I am driftwood on his beach,
without an uncle or a radio.
I used to be a Spanish ship.
Thinking of Seville, mahogany,
he picks me up
feeling both superior and sorry.

✲ ✲ ✲

Or I am brave and he is smaller
than the smallest thing
he can remember.
They had him sit for hours
on a chair; they had him
in there with the flies.
I am opening all the doors, now
I call up the authorities
and say, *Here, look at this*
and that. I am standing there,
my hair righteously undone
and smiling down. He hates me.
He's excited.

✲ ✲ ✲

We are upside down in spoons.
In the morning we exchange
our dreams for nervous chatter.
I dreamt I was the cat you loved.
Something spills.
Someone makes a graceful leap
for rags. Someone mutters, *clumsy.*

Lily's marking stock in the back
where Walter sweeps and bets
and makes boxes out of cardboard.
Rose at the cash dreams Cracow.
She's got numbers on her arm. Eleanor
threatens to call the union
if my father calls her fat once more.
She's fat.

The code for thieves is nineteen;
when Pauline shouts *nineteen* aloud
everyone's eyes go *where* until they fall
on Pauline crooning *May I help you?*
to someone in a big coat.
A pig could fit in there.

Lily knows her husband is a bum.
She's marking stock and time, telling him
in her head he can go to hell with his blonde
for all she cares. She's hungry, too.
New goods are coming in!
Walter heaves the cartons down the stairs.
As my father dares him to be careful,
Walter slaps the stuff across the racks: scarves
and slacks, blouses from Hong Kong
made wrong and all

to be discounted, men's furnishings
only in one color, thin silk dresses for a party,
for an evening, for a song—
these stunning, damaged things.

If you're the bad and never-minding pony,
then I'm the niece in organdy.
That narrow man? He's my master of the dance
who wants me staying still. He wants everything
in almost silence.
                                        If you're the laggard liar boy,
then I'm the vole of meanest teeth, the snarl
and laughter of a daughter too American:
That's not the way you say it, Daddy.
                                        How did we come together
if you're the yellow hills and grasses, the wolf
inside the moon, while I'm the view of the hotel?
                                        Here's the porch,
the empty wicker creel tilted on the steps, a girl
who dreams that rectitude is vengeance.

By the end of this poem I will lie.
If I dared to, in cold light,
I could decipher my dreams. *If you cared to,*
if you saw what I was driving at,
I can hear him swearing yesterday,
and tomorrow hear him say the same.
                                        We are so much the way we are.

I am not lying yet.
Now it is the war; laughing, there are sailors
I am waving to. Yesterday is all those years ago
and years when, in the car, my father turns to me
his anger by the way he brakes.
And forgives me his distraction when I hit my head.

I say I am sorry too.

Over the telephone poles the birds fly.
Over the solar and the modular paper-walled cottages
and their plum trees. It is afternoon.

Now the girls prepare a charcoal fire for the tea
while the boys climb down from trees
to greet their fathers who are hot;
their planes were hot, the airport crowded.

And the mothers search the tumble in the laundry
for a cloth to spread across the table
lately covered with books and cigarettes
and letters: *. . . we have arrived; your visa will expire. . .*

Does it matter how the boiled water pours into a bowl?
The tea is new and powdered. The ritual is old.
Does it matter that it happens in a circle?

When night purrs on electrically,
the girls change back to jeans; the boys
stumble on the untied laces of their running shoes.
They weave around the house. The ceremony's over.
All of them go flying through the rooms.

It is 1434. Jan van Eyck begins
to paint the merchant and his wife.
It is a witness of their marriage,
said to be a rebus of that event
full of medieval symbols.
He paints them in their bedroom.
He shows a leaded window, a peach
ripening on the sill. That fruit
represents the bliss before the fall.
The Passion of the Lord
is in the mirror frame in miniature.
Almost everything is small: the dog,
her timid smile,
their respective pairs of slippers.

It is 1434. When van Eyck tries
the new perspective,
the man and wife seem large
for the scale of the room.
They are noble only by their clothes;
her dress, voluminous and green,
his hat which seems enormous.
The setting is less glorious than familiar.
While natural light comes through
the open window, an individual candle burns.
It is human caprice that flickers,
flickers and steadies and shines.

Probably you already know
how the world is made cruel
mainly by comparisons,
and how, in your most equable times,
you will notice this
on crowded streets where the gifted go along
with those totally lacking in luster,
and probably you will grieve, and grieve
for the times when grief is not with you

when you are happy walking
with your undiscovered woman
distractingly fair-skinned and able.
When you are bored with all of this pleasure,
you can turn on her with mean words
or have her turn on you, or turn away.
And one day a white peony crawled with ants
will be whiter than one entirely clean.

There will be a table, a workplace.
You will be sitting there,
more or less successfully plotting
the stars and the accounts received for them.
You will have mild nights, your children's
real dreams of storms and more than one
pair of shoes used up and cracked.
You will not throw the shoes away
saying *Done with you.* Nothing is done in memory.

Every spring the buds will insist
you put aside what you don't yet know
about choices: how many are wrong, how few

are the incomparable right ones,
and about what does and does not matter
here on earth where you will have, finally,
no choice at all
and where your death will compare to nothing.

What I know
is this skin-covered cask
I call my body, these staves: ribs
the cooper made in a day from dust.

What I know are mountains grinding
down to sand: an eroding beach
sadly flanked by tatter
that's called scrub.

Gulls bicker and chatter and fly
so noisily above the crossroad bustle
where an arch and spire dicker
over time.

It's a baby in the wind dabbing rings
across the pond: circles
fed by springs I cannot see...
Oblivion jeers but it's nothing.

who stole feathers from the swans
and mocked her little sister with the devil
drew one awkward rose
over and over the pages of her copybook.

                    Fat and beautiful,
she flew in jewels to Texas for a cure,
fainted in the heat and telegrammed for cash.
Wasting that, she then came home ashamed.

                    Constantly about to die,
this woman rummaging through my things, my life
as if it were an open bin, calls to say

next week she cruises up the Nile
on nothing but nougat and bottled water
and do I want some money and am I smoking still

                    and do I know her hands
and feet are turning blue and brilliant
crimson swiftly changeable and yes, I say, I do.

It is the dream house; it is the holidays.
Everything is ribbons, spruce festoons
the halls I am escorted through.
I hear the music of politeness, flutes,
the music of certain orders.
                                        I am escorted through the rooms
and at the last the bath is lavender: the fixtures
of the tub and sink are crystal swans
                                            so filthy I am shocked.
In that room they have my mother's vases
and a scale as black as dirt when it is rich,
and I have to weigh myself; they say
they want to see my pleasing little body.

✲ ✲ ✲

I am tired of dread, of three bears
who stand beside my bed at dawn, calling,
Rude, rude, you've broken things.
Wedded to the woodsman now, I can refuse
the wolf his due; the heartless queen
is very old. It was years and long ago
she wanted my heart with salt.
                                            In the new house
with the blue rug the color of the sea,
I keep a child. In dreams he's lost.
In snow he thinks the windows look like sugar.
Luck he chooses, luck and silver pebbles.

They meant only to be kind.
Cakes were passed, sweet cakes
with poppy seeds.
Someone handed me a coffee.
There was a girl; there were smiles
all around, and a fire in the grate
made shadows. Could I explain?
It was Sunday, all day, rain.

Might I have told a soul
about the shadows? They seemed
like dogs, too fond, so very big –
I dropped my spoon.
And from them such solicitude
I could have wept but shrugged

instead, inept, without a word of praise
for the food and the ordinary beauty
of the cupboard. The girl –
little star, all glitter
and white night
come to blister my sleep, I wish.
They had lilac, asters, painted
on the dishes. I left. No irony
walks on these wet streets.
The twitting birds – they humble me.

I shall be heard by the spheres!

He lives between a sonnet and a war.
This is always so, although less clear
to those of us upset by shirts
or the days of gray: late March
when scruff predominates, collecting
in the nap of a turkey carpet. A wife
again is lying down.

He gambles, and walks her, for the view,
up a little hill, then down again. Probably
she stumbles; sweeping round the knoll,
she is so intense she cries,
This is godly yellow scrim,
and later in their bed says out loud
White is my protection. He says, *little hill*
and climbs in sleep, climbs down.

And never wakes from it: love,
that half-respect, half-hatred
for the private door threatening
to close. In the final years
he plants some iris, balm
against the real hell that lives inside her radio.
Leonard Woolf. Used and taken only as example.

They are in there, all the souls:
dinosaurs, butcher kings, queens who promise
night's best whispers, and girls
fixed to the relentless
footfalls of the moon. Behind the heart:
saints and a pack
of flowers blooming mightily, like pity.

So the blood goes through
a million small blue salty rivers.
So the spine goes cracking, ticking.
And full of years, the breath,
the inspiration, sighs, expires, sighs...

They are in there: narrow flukes, the plucky
flint-struck ancestors moving
like ignited ones toward an appointment with desire.
Big bang, go the cool brain's tiny fires.

Everything is something else; the sky is
grit once bone and flesh, dog and master,
a lover and his bride
wishing that the sky be night forever.

                                        The sky will be
my husband gone to work carrying his tools
and his mother in his brain.
                                        His head aches. She is angry.

                                        Birds are lighter kin.
The cardinal, canted, dancing at the feeder,
has been my uncle drunk on holidays,
and my father, who controlled from terror,
is the fearful jay.
                                        He patrols the spruce.

I dream I stand in Einstein's time; the sky is
filled with fishing birds ascending
                                        from the fish that spawned them.
The spume off the bay is feathers.
                                        I dream nothing could ever hurt me.

Ghost crabs hide from the tide.

Because justice cannot be
without a crime, in bed
we reinvent the perfect one.
How fair we are in the lamplight.

✲ ✲ ✲

We will never get to Italy.
Snow has buried the terrace
once again. We will never get to Paris,
we will never be loved

the way we think we need to be: completely
with complete attention. In the evening
the windowpanes are Tuscan glass,
imperfect deep Provençal blue.

Our shoes are soldiers' boots.

When I was a fool, history had answers.
Now I drink with my friend.
She tells me how her mother, long ago
beautiful in black, was wounded
by her father. What he said was terrible.

I was confused by Russia and dizzy
thinking of twenty million horses decomposing
in the sun next to Catherine's wedding dress
and one cup of blue enameled hexagons.
Catherine annexed the whole Crimea.
She gained the Baltic ports, reined her serfs
so hard they almost choked, and wrote this
of her lover: . . . *he leaps like a buck in air;*
his eyes which shine like torches throw off sparks.

My friend looking for a reason in her past
sees her mother on the stairs, at dusk, coming up
or going down. When I was a fool I had to know
where people stood. It was a way of fixing things.

I look in memory: there's an apple.
I look at my hands: here's the core.
Too many floors wear the tread
of hundreds of people already dust; too many
bachelors sighing
She'll come, my rose, my girl,
have wintered with a blasted wife.
Mozart loves Constanze!
But the Austrian court, how dumb it is...
silk stretched beyond its limits
frays, simply disappears.

My friends are slides and I project them
on a wall painted white over blue
over paper: someone's cool idea
of lacy vines *inside.*
My friends are still nineteen, caught up
in will that will catch itself in circumstance.
Blossoms. Fading without darkness in the light.

I look in memory: there's a love.
Here in my hands is his letter: he was mine
and now he's sorry...
Look how Mozart paces!
Listen to the curtains; listen to the notes
the snow erases. I sleep and dream
I'm breathing. At dawn: the color of apples.

Light falls on the cup and the plate,
fluted spoons, the blue in the milk,
salt, the half-eaten egg, the table,
someone half dreaming. Light falls on the clock.

Light falls on our uncles the fish,
on disguise, on sleight-of-hand,
on doctors with shaky investments.
It falls on the mess of the willow,
mistakes in the garden: too many roses,
on children allergic to bees, their fathers
in terror through summer, on a body
all out of breath.

Light plays on the righteous,
on waste, on the harvest of insistent arrangers,
on obsession, on justification: that dance
designed in the mind;
in the water
light copies the reeds bending and weaving,
and it falls on the roofs of houses,
little houses resting on ground
that was, just moments ago, submerged by the sea.
Light travels that fast.
It falls on me. Just moments ago
I had no vision at all.

Looking like an angel, the angel
who makes me sigh and sad about my age
has gone to a rock concert down in Providence.

I think he got bored with the beach,
and me loving the extravagance
of an early summer garden without a thought
of rot, that terrible twin of affluence.

Anyway he's taken the tuna and white wine
and I ought to give him hell but I can't.
Providence is hell, hot with impossible traffic.

And he'll be back. The poem is that he went away.

If the woman languishing
on the terrace chair seems indolent,
her upturned hands unscarred
and the milk jug full on the nearby table,
graceful in its leg, turned, cabriole;
if she seems wistful, recollecting
such perfume as is offered by the opening grove
of lilac or the man she begged who went away;
if she cries, if she bends watching ants
busy on the bricks or the bricks themselves,
the multi-hues of pink or, in between, moss
arranging itself in herringbone,
think how random it is: lust; that friend
slashing all her dresses then her skin,
the usually innocent children and nobody
to bring a glass of water —
how blackbirds, complaining, hover
on southern scrub and sing, their red wing-bars
always such a shock, the ordinary blossoms
wild in the shade and a whole blue sky.

The Author

Caroline Finkelstein was born in New York City. Awards for her poetry include a grant from the Vermont Council on the Arts and a National Endowment for the Arts fellowship for 1984. She lives in Rochester, Massachusetts, with her family.

Photograph by Robert Clinton